HOW INDIA IS GOVERNED

HOW INDIA IS GOVERNED:

BEING AN ACCOUNT OF

ENGLAND'S WORK IN INDIA

ALEXANDER MACKENZIE

GYAN

Published by

GYAN

Gyan Publishing House
5, Ansari Road
Daryaganj, New Delhi-110002
Phone: 011-47034999, 9811692060
E-mail: books@gyanbooks.com

Distribution Network
gyanbooks.com
India, USA, Canada, UK, Australia

ISBN: 978-93-7097-521-7 (PB)

First Published, 1882

2nd Impression 2025

Printed at: Gyan Press, Delhi.

**HOW INDIA IS GOVERNED:
BEING AN ACCOUNT OF ENGLAND'S WORK IN INDIA**
Author: ALEXANDER MACKENZIE

HOW INDIA IS GOVERNED

HOW INDIA IS GOVERNED

BEING AN ACCOUNT OF

ENGLAND'S WORK IN INDIA

BY

ALEXANDER MACKENZIE

LATE MEMBER OF THE LEGISLATIVE COUNCIL, MADRAS

LONDON

KEGAN PAUL, TRENCH & CO., 1, PATERNOSTER SQUARE

1882

PREFACE.

For the convenience of English readers I have in these pages expressed money figures in sterling instead of in Indian currency.

For the information about native states which I have tabulated in the appendix, I am largely indebted to Mr. Loke Nath Ghose's interesting "History of the Indian Chiefs and Rajahs."

A. MACKENZIE.

CONTENTS.

APPENDIX.

ENGLAND'S WORK IN INDIA.

THERE are few things which so immediately and so painfully impress an Englishman on returning from India to his native land as the general paucity of information, among his countrymen, on England's work in the East. The magnitude, and even the interest as an experiment, of the gigantic task which England has accepted appears to be wholly unappreciated. But surely the labour of introducing among an alien population, whose numbers amount to nearly one-sixth of the entire human race, and include almost as many varieties of character and language as the continent of Europe, a settled system of government founded on the latest convictions of the statesman and the philanthropist, and simultaneous efforts to develope the industrial resources of the country, and to supply to a poor and widely scattered populace such appliances of civilization as may ameliorate its condition and increase its prosperity, should, and would if properly apprehended, receive a closer and more intelligent attention. To excite such attention, we do not require histories of the leading wars and similar incidents which have produced the Indian Empire. We have to deal with subjects which concern the daily life of the people, and with the work which for many years past has been silently and conscientiously carried on by our countrymen in a foreign land, among alien and distrustful races; it may truly be said, without notice or expression of interest or approval from that British public whose national honour is so deeply concerned in the results of their labours.

It is in the hope that a short account of what has been, and is still being, done for the fulfilment of this great work may not be without effect in rousing my countrymen to greater interest in it, that I have ventured to publish the following chapters. I have endeavoured to condense each subject into as brief a compass as possible; to avoid wearying the general reader by columns of statistics of little interest except to specialists; and to confine the information given to a description of broad principles and average results.

I have not written for the already well-informed and practical statistician, but for those to whom at present our Indian system of government and social administration is an unfamiliar subject; and to such I venture to think the information given will be found useful and not uninteresting.

RISE AND PROGRESS OF THE INDIAN EMPIRE.

THE origin of the East India Company, to which may justly be attributed the formation of our Indian empire, was an association of private merchants, styled "The Governor and Company of Merchants of London trading into the East Indies." This company was instituted A.D. 1600, with a capital of £72,000, and got by charter from the Crown the monopoly of trade with the East Indies. Its agents established depôts—or factories, as they were called—in various parts of India, which, after a short time, were fortified and garrisoned; and thus a footing in the country was acquired, which speedily led to schemes for territorial dominion quite at variance with the objects professed by the united traders.

In 1612 permission was obtained from the Court at Delhi to establish a factory at Surat; and this was quickly followed by settlements in other parts of India. Fort St. George (Madras) was established in 1640, and in 1645 various settlements, of which Hoogly was the chief, were commenced in Bengal. These were at that time subordinate to Madras. The original charter was renewed by Cromwell in 1657, and confirmed by Charles II. in 1661, with various important privileges of exercising civil and criminal jurisdiction, and other rights of a sovereign power, in the Company's possessions. In 1677 another renewal of the charter was obtained, with permission to establish a mint at Bombay. Meanwhile, many private adventurers had entered into the trade, in contravention of the exclusive rights granted by the charter to the Company, and much dispute and difficulty had thereby been occasioned. In 1693 a further renewal of the charter and its trading monopolies was granted by the Crown, but in 1694 the House of Commons passed a resolution, "That all the subjects of England have an equal right to trade to the East Indies, unless prohibited by Act of Parliament;" and in 1698 a second Company obtained a charter from the legislature, conferring upon it also the *exclusive* right of trade with the East Indies. In 1708 the two companies amalgamated under the style of "The United Company of Merchants of England trading to the East Indies," and the union was duly ratified and confirmed by Parliament. Meanwhile, the Bengal agency had been established at Calcutta, and Fort William had been built. From 1715 to 1717, various privileges were, under treaty, conferred by the Mogul Court at Delhi upon the Company, all tending to confirm and establish its position in the country. Treaties with the Nabob of the Carnatic, and victory in the Company's struggle with the French for supremacy in Southern India, placed a large part of the Madras Presidency under its control; and the battle of Plassey, in 1757, wrested the provinces of Bengal, Behar, and Orissa from the Mogul emperor. But these continued wars and intrigues had excited attention in England, and in 1782 the House of Commons passed a resolution, "That to pursue schemes of conquest and extent of dominion in India are measures repugnant to the wish, the honour, and the policy of this nation." In pursuance of the principle thus enunciated, Mr. Fox at once introduced a bill to amend the special privileges granted to the Company, and to place the Government of India under Commissioners to be appointed by Parliament. The bill was, amid great excitement and opposition, passed by the House of Commons, but rejected by the House of Lords. A change of Ministry followed in consequence, and Mr. Pitt brought forward a bill which was accepted by both Houses, and which fixed the constitution of the East India Company until its abolition in 1858. The chief principle of this bill was the formation of the "Board of Control," composed of six members of the Privy Council, for the special supervision of all matters concerning the civil or military government or revenues of the territories in possession of the East India Company; and the appointment of a special tribunal for the trial in England of all British subjects accused of important offences or misconduct committed in India. The conduct of commercial affairs and matters of minor importance remained, as before, with the directors.

Under the administrations of the Marquis Cornwallis and the Marquis Wellesley, the Company's possessions were largely increased by conquest in various directions, and by the cession of large territories by the Mahratta chiefs. But the accessions of revenue, large as they were, from the new possessions were insufficient to meet the continued increase of expenditure, and the result was a constant accumulation of debt. It is not surprising, therefore, that, during the early years of this century, attention should have been attracted to the generally unprofitable result of the trading monopoly granted to the Company; and, after long agitation, the privilege of free trade with Hindostan was thrown open, in 1813, to the general public. The result was so marked, the aggregate of trade in the first five years from this concession having augmented some fourfold, that it was impossible any longer to defend the monopoly, and, as it soon became evident that the Company could not compete in commerce with the private traders, the stockholders resolved, in 1834, to close its commercial business. From that date until 1858 the Company confined itself to the administration of its vast territories, which were further increased by the conquest of Scinde in 1845, of the Punjaub in 1849, and of Pegu and Martaban in Burmah in 1852. The constantly increasing magnitude and importance of the dominion thus almost insensibly acquired, and the heavy responsibilities which were being placed in effect upon the British nation, could not fail to attract attention. It was felt to be an anomaly that questions of national interest should be left to the direction of individuals, instead of to that of the nation, and the opinions and sentiments which were daily gaining ground and expression were brought into action by the sepoy mutiny of 1857. A bill was at once passed for transferring the government of India from the Company to the Crown; and thus, after an existence of two and a half centuries, terminated the East India Company, the most remarkable record which the world affords of great and unexpected results from small beginnings.

AREA AND POPULATION.

HINDOSTAN comprises two main divisions—British India, or the territories under the direct management of the Indian Government; and the Native States which are in the actual possession of their several princes, who exercise therein all such rights of a sovereign power as are usually conceded by a suzerain to his feudatory.

British India is estimated to contain a grand total of 869,951 square miles, with a population of 184,898,867, distributed as follows :—

		Square miles.		Population.
Bengal	...	607,176	......	137,388,916
Madras	...	138,318	......	31,281,177
Bombay	...	124,457	......	16,228,774

It should, however, be explained that in this summary the term "Bengal" includes the minor provinces of British Burmah, Assam, the Punjaub, the North-West Provinces and Oudh, the Central Provinces, as well as Bengal proper. The figures of area and population for these different districts are as follows :—

	Square miles.		Population.
Bengal proper ...	189,034	......	62,724,840
The Punjaub ...	98,461	......	17,604,505
North-West Provinces	81,402	......	30,774,056
Oudh ...	24,069	......	11,197,266
Central Provinces ...	84,048	......	8,215,167
Assam ...	41,798	......	4,132,019
British Burmah ...	88,364	......	2,741,063

The Native States contain an estimated area of 650,000 square miles, and a population estimated at fifty to fifty-five millions. The information at public disposal regarding many of the minor states is somewhat imperfect. A list of the chief native states, with particulars of area, revenue, and population, will be found in the Appendix.

THE INDIAN CONSTITUTION.

THE administration of government in India is primarily under the sovereign of Great Britain, through Parliament; but the actual machinery in England is the Secretary of State and Council, located at Westminster, who may be considered the chief administrative power. Next in degree come the Viceroy and his Council, and then the Governors of Madras and Bombay, and the Lieutenant-Governors of Bengal, the North-West Provinces, and the Punjaub, with their respective Councils. A short summary of the constitution of each body will be of service.

HOME GOVERNMENT.—The Secretary of State for India is a member of the Ministry for the time being, and therefore each change of Ministry involves a change in the State Secretaryship; an arrangement not without grave disadvantages in the government of a country where so much is still in an unsettled, or partially settled, condition.

He has a Council of fifteen members, who retain office "during good behaviour." Each receives a salary of £1200 per annum. All the home business of India is conducted by this Council and the establishment under their control at Westminster; for example, engagement of officers for various departments of Indian civil administration, payments of pensions, provision of funds for Indian expenditure in England, negotiations with the railway companies, purchase of stores for Indian administrative requirements, and similar matters.

The Secretary of State has the power of "vetoing" any legislative enactment or administrative arrangement of the Viceroy and his Council, and even, in cases of emergency, the power of overriding the decisions of his own Council. It is to be assumed that in this respect his position is intended to be analogous to that of the Crown towards Parliament; and, in fact, that such supreme powers are only to be exercised under the direction of the Crown or its constitutional advisers.

SUPREME GOVERNMENT OF INDIA.—The Viceroy is appointed, as vacancies occur, by the sovereign, in concert with the constitutional advisers of the Crown. He is usually a member of the party for the time being in power, but does not necessarily vacate on a change of Ministry. He holds office for five years. The seat of government is nominally Calcutta, but of late years it has been the custom for the Viceroys and the Council to spend the greater part of the year at Simla. The Viceroy, or, as he is more generally styled in business matters, the Governor-General of India, is assisted by a Council of six ordinary members, the Commander-in-Chief, and the Lieutenant-Governor of Bengal. The ordinary members are appointed by himself, under confirmation of the Crown, and hold office for five years. This body is known as the Supreme Council. He has also a Council for the purpose of making laws, known as the Supreme Legislative Council, composed of the members of the Supreme Council and nine others, of whom five must be non-official, that is, not holding any office under Government, and presumably independent of Government influence. No salary attaches to these latter appointments.

The Supreme Council possesses a control (largely exercised in matters of finance) over the subordinate or provincial Governments, in all important matters of administration; and has the power of amending or cancelling any orders or proceedings of such subordinate Governments.

The Supreme Legislative Council undertakes the provision of laws applicable to the Empire generally, leaving the passage of local Acts to the provincial legislative bodies.

Provincial Governments.—These are five in number, viz. Madras, Bombay, Bengal, North-West Provinces, Punjaub. Each, though ultimately subordinate to the Supreme Government, has independent administration of its territory and finances, with distinct establishments of Civil, Revenue, and Judicial officers. The first two have also separate military establishments; but the last three are associated with the Bengal army system.

GOVERNMENT OF MADRAS.—The Governor, like the Viceroy, is appointed direct by the Crown. He holds office for five years. His head-quarters are at Madras, but the incumbent usually spends much of the year, with his Council, etc., on the Neilgherry Hills. He is assisted by a Council of three, viz. the Commander-in-Chief, and two members of the Civil Service appointed by the Governor himself, under confirmation by the Crown. The Commander-in-Chief is *ex-officio* a member during his tenure of the military command, but he takes little part in the civil administrative work of the Council. The civilian members hold office for five years. There is also a Legislative Council for the manufacture of laws applicable specially to the province, composed of the Executive Council and eight other members, of whom not less than six must be non-officials. No Act can be introduced for consideration until the draft has been approved by the Viceroy; and every Act passed by the Council must receive the consent of the Viceroy before it becomes law and can be placed on the local statute book. The non-official members of the Council hold office for two years, but are eligible for reappointment. They do not receive any salary or allowances.

GOVERNMENT OF BOMBAY.—The Governor is appointed in the manner and under the conditions described in the case of Madras. His head-quarters are at Bombay, but during the hot-weather months an exodus usually takes place to some one of the hill stations on the "Western Ghauts," or hill ranges. His Executive and Legislative Councils are formed on the same principles and under the same regulations as those of the Madras Presidency.

GOVERNMENT OF BENGAL.—Bengal is administered by a Lieutenant-Governor, with a Legislative Council of twelve members, of whom six must be non-officials. The regulations for tenure of office and despatch of business in this Council are similar to those in force at Madras and Bombay.

The Lieutenant-Governor is appointed by the Viceroy, and holds office for five years. Head-quarters are at Calcutta.

The military establishment is directly under the Government of India, but it is known as the Bengal army, and provides forces not only for that province, but also for the North-West Provinces and the Punjaub.

THE NORTH-WEST PROVINCES AND THE PUN-

JAUB are respectively under the charge of a Lieutenant-Governor appointed by the Viceroy, who holds office for five years. The military forces of these districts are drawn from the Bengal army.

DEPARTMENTAL SYSTEM.—The chief burden of the executive or departmental work of the Empire falls upon the Indian Civil Service, which is divided into two main divisions of covenanted and uncovenanted servants of Government, or, in other words, those to whom are secured, by terms of their appointment, certain exclusive privileges and emoluments, and those whose appointments are of a more temporary and less lucrative nature.

The Covenanted Civil Service, as it now exists, is the final development of the mercantile establishment of clerks, etc., created by the East India Company for the purposes of its trade with India. As the Company gradually acquired territory, certain members of the mercantile establishment were transferred from the trading depôts to the work of collecting rents, and other duties of a land agent on a large property; and as more and more of the country fell into the hands of the Company, necessity arose to provide permanently, not only for the collection of rents or land revenue and the maintenance of irrigation works, roads, etc., but for the administration of justice in both civil and criminal cases, and the regulation generally of the social affairs of the country. Such duties, it was evident, would require a class of gentlemen of considerable attainments and unquestionable probity; and it would be necessary to offer pecuniary inducements and a social position sufficient to attract young men of ability and family, who would naturally demand guarantees of permanent, profitable, and honourable employment.

Without giving details of the various arrangements of the East India Company for carrying out their object, it will suffice to say the gentlemen specially selected and trained for the Civil Service of India were secured, by written agreement, certain emoluments of pay and pension, and the exclusive right to the chief appointments in the Government machinery. From this form of agreement, or "covenant," the distinctive title of "Covenanted Civil Service" originated; and although the system of direct appointments and special education adopted by the East India Company has been abandoned for one more popular in the present day—that of competitive examinations, the service still retains its distinctive character of a privileged body. The Uncovenanted Service was in former days chiefly composed of natives and "East Indians" (or the descendants of the early European residents by native mothers), and did little more than supply clerks for the various public offices, subordinate district officers, etc., etc.; but of late years, owing to the great extension of the Government schemes for improving and developing the resources of the country, it has been largely recruited by Europeans of considerable professional attainments, and at this moment includes many men certainly not inferior in education and ability to their more fortunate brethren of the Covenanted Service. A large proportion of the Uncovenanted Civil Service is employed as clerks in the different Government secretariats and public offices; others in the Educational Department, Telegraphs, Forests, Canals, State Railways, and other departments of the public works; but the bulk of the service fills the minor administrative posts of the revenue and judicial services.

The work of covenanted civilians may be divided into the two main heads of Revenue and Judicial administration. Under the former is comprised the collection of land rent and all taxes and Government dues, and the control of all matters of irrigation, communication, and social interest; under the latter, the administration of justice throughout the country. As a general rule, a young civilian, on arriving in India, or shortly afterwards, elects to which branch of the service he will specially devote himself, and it is not usual to transfer men experienced in revenue or district work to a judgeship, or *vice versâ*. The principle of the internal or subordinate government of the Empire is by division into districts or departments, each complete in its revenue, and judicial, staff. Each district is under the charge of a senior civilian, known in some Presidencies as Collector, in others as Commissioner. Under him, located in different parts of the district, are a Sub-Collector and usually two junior or Assistant Collectors, all belonging to the Covenanted Service, and a large staff of "uncovenanted" deputies and petty district and village officers. All the covenanted, and a large proportion of the uncovenanted, staff possess magisterial powers, and hold the courts of first enquiry in criminal matters. The Collector is the chief Government authority in the district, and takes official precedence of the Judge, even though this latter should be his senior in the service—a vestige, no doubt, of the days when the East India Company was a trading institution, and considered provision of income the most important duty entrusted to its servants.

The main part of the Collector's duties is in connection with the land revenue, which, speaking roughly, may be said to provide one-half of the settled revenues of the country (see chapter on Land Revenue). He has further the collections of all special taxes, and of cesses imposed for local purposes, such as education, maintenance of highways, etc. The irrigation and communication works of the district are under his control, with a special engineering staff for construction and maintenance; and, in short, to be an efficient district officer a man requires considerable physical and mental powers; for the districts range in extent from 3000 to as much as 11,000 square miles, with populations of from 500,000 to over two millions, and a good district officer is expected to make, and keep, himself acquainted with the conditions and circumstances of the people, prospects of crops, etc., and to report to the Government of his Presidency periodically on all subjects of interest.

Each district has a Chief Court, presided over by a covenanted civilian, known as a "Civil and Sessions Judge." He sits daily for ten months of the year, and the greater part of his time is occupied in civil cases; but he holds periodical sessions of gaol delivery for trial of criminal offenders committed by the various magistrates of the district. An appeal against his decision, in both civil and criminal cases, can be made to the High Court of the Presidency in which his district is situated; and in important civil cases a further appeal lies from such High Court to the Judicial Committee of the Privy Council. Many large districts have "Small Cause Courts," also presided over by a covenanted civilian, for the trial of minor civil cases. The district courts have probate jurisdiction under certain limitations.

Jurisdiction in cases of bankruptcy can only be exercised by district courts in cases where the debtor has been arrested by a judgment creditor and has applied to the court to take charge of his property and relieve him from arrest. Failing such arrest, a debtor in the "up-country" districts is powerless to obtain relief by declaring himself bankrupt, or to prevent the first creditors who may succeed in attaching his property from paying themselves in full, to the prejudice of creditors at a distance.

In the chief Presidency towns—say Calcutta, Madras, Bombay, Allahabad, Lahore—High

Courts are established for the despatch not only of local civil or criminal business, but, as stated above, with appellate jurisdiction over the proceedings of the subordinate district courts. The constitution of these courts is as follows :—

BENGAL (CALCUTTA).

1 Chief Justice on Rs. 6000 per month.
11 Puisne Judges on Rs. 4166 „

MADRAS.

1 Chief Justice on Rs. 5000 per month.
4 Puisne Judges on Rs. 3750 „

BOMBAY.

1 Chief Justice on Rs. 5000 per month.
7 Puisne Judges on Rs. 3750 „

NORTH-WEST PROVINCES AND OUDH (ALLAHABAD).

5 Judges of the High Court, average pay about Rs. 4000 per month.

PUNJAUB (LAHORE).

3 Judges of the High Court, average pay about Rs. 4000 per month.

BRITISH BURMAH.

1 Recorder and 1 Judicial Commissioner.

Details of the subordinate establishments of Civil and Sessions District Courts, Small Cause Courts, and Magistrates' Courts throughout the country, would be too voluminous for the limits of this work.

The High Courts are of great influence in the

administration of justice throughout the Empire. They have the sole privilege of trying European British subjects for all serious criminal offences; and the importance attached by the natives to the right of appeal to the High Court from the decisions of the district courts cannot be overestimated. Nor can such a state of native opinion be fairly considered uncalled for. The civilians who preside over the district courts are not, as a rule, possessed of any great legal training or knowledge beyond what they have succeeded in mastering in the course of their Indian service. With comparatively few exceptions, they have not, prior to leaving England, been called to the bar, or even kept terms at any Inns of Court, while many of the cases which come before them for decision involve most complicated questions of common and statute law, as well as of Hindoo and Mahometan usage. In addition to these disadvantages, there are constant transfers from one district to another, caused by the conditions of the service, *e g.* promotion on retirement of senior officers, absences on sick leave or furlough, etc., etc.; so that it is now unusual for an officer to spend such length of time in one district as would familiarize him with the local usages, the peculiarities of his subordinate magistrates (themselves frequently changed), and other matters affecting the conduct of business in his district which it is desirable he should master. It may well be doubted whether the present system of supplying the district courts from the ranks of the Covenanted Civil Service is the best which could be devised, and whether such appointments might not now, under the altered conditions of the country, be thrown open to the English bar under a system of selection by the Home Government — each special appointment to be held permanently by the incumbent for a definite period of service.

The High Courts possess probate and insolvency jurisdiction (the latter only for residents of the town where the court has its seat), and their judges are usually called upon to advise the Legislative Councils on drafts of Acts which it may be proposed to pass into law.

Covenanted civilians are usually selected by the local Governments for any appointments of administrative importance not appertaining to the special departments of district work, such as Collector of sea customs, Postmaster-General, Commissioners of salt or opium revenue, etc.

There are also special prizes of the service, such as the head-quarter Secretaryships, and seats on Boards of Revenue and Provincial and Supreme Councils, the offices of Comptrollers of accounts, provincial Accountant-Generals, Foreign Office appointments, etc., which are held to fall by right of service to the senior members of the covenanted class of civilians.

The total number of covenanted civilians now on the effective lists is rather over 900, of whom about 160 are of the old service of "Haileybury men," and the remainder have gained their appointments under the "competition" system. Of these 900, about 600 are employed in Bengal and the provinces immediately in relation with it, about 160 in Madras, and 140 in Bombay.

The rates of pay in the junior branches range from about £400 to £1200 per annum. Senior district officers, such as Collectors and Judges, get from £2400 to £3000 per annum. Special appointments range from £3000 up to £10,000. Nearly 100, or about ten per cent. of the total number of civilians, draw over £3000 per annum.

A covenanted civilian is entitled, after twenty-one years' actual service in India, to a pension of £1000 per annum. Service for smaller periods entitles to pension on lower scales.

An uncovenanted civilian is not entitled to any pension until after fifteen years' service, but only to a gratuity of one month's pay for each year of service. After service of over fifteen but less than twenty-five years, he can claim a pension not exceeding one-third of the average pay drawn during his service; and after twenty-five years a pension not exceeding one-half of such average pay.

In addition to the special revenue and judicial duties discharged by the covenanted and uncovenanted civilians, there is a vast organization of subsidiary departments carried on by special agency, under the control, more or less direct, of the head-quarter and subordinate Governments of each Presidency. Such are, for example, the departments of Salt, Opium, Excise, Stamps, Forests, Irrigation, Public Works, Education, Railways, etc., etc. In fact, to realize the position of the Government of India, the reader must endeavour to imagine what would be the position of the English Government if every landlord were to renounce his duties as an owner of property, and to throw upon the Home Office the task of providing for and supervising every detail on which the public safety and the social comfort of the country depend.

LEGISLATION.

THE members of the trading parties originally sent out by the East India Company were, of necessity, subject to the judicial tribunals of the native rulers; but the Company took early opportunity of obtaining a "commission under the Great Seal" from the Crown of England, which empowered the presidents of the factories to try British subjects for criminal offences by "martial law," and to inflict even capital sentences. All civil disputes between Europeans appear to have been decided by the chiefs of the factories. Cases of dispute, either civil or criminal, between Europeans and natives were still subject to the native tribunals.

The charter of 1661 gave the governors and councils of the several factories power to exercise civil and criminal jurisdiction in their respective charges "according to the laws of England." In 1669 the East India Company obtained a special grant or power to pass "laws and constitutions for the good government of the settlement" of Bombay, and to inflict necessary punishments. Such laws were to be "as near as may be agreeable to" the laws of England; and any person sentenced under them to the penalty of death was to have a right of appeal to the Crown of England.

Early in the eighteenth century the Company appears to have established, in all chief settlements, "Mayor's Courts," composed of a mayor and nine aldermen, who adjudicated upon all minor civil and criminal disputes, and from whose decision there was an appeal to the governor and council of the factory.

But as the Company acquired territory, and became in fact rulers of a great part of Hindostan, the question of judicial administration became very serious. The laws of England were not suited to the customs and usages of Hindoos and Mahometans; and as the Company's servants began to realize their new position in the country, and to get greater insight into the social life of the people, they recognized the necessity of accepting the native law codes, such as they were, whenever these were compatible with recognized principles of equity and morality.

About 1770, therefore, as a first step towards what was needed, the Company appointed, in each district under its control a Civil and a Criminal Court, with Courts of Appeal at the chief seats of government; and drew up a code of "Regulations," as they were styled, but which were in fact intended to be, so far as they extended, statute law, for the guidance of the presidents of such courts. In continuation of the work thus commenced, the Company obtained, in 1773, a special Act of Parliament (13 Geo. III.), by which, among other matters, special power was given to the Governor-General of India and his Council "to make and issue such rules, ordinances, and regulations for the good order and civil government of the settlement of Fort William and other factories subordinate, or to be subordinate, thereto, as shall be deemed just and reasonable; such rules, ordinances, and regulations not being repugnant to the laws of the Realm." This Act practically inaugurated the formation of a distinct Statute Book for India, and under its authority the work of legislation was carried on by the Council until 1833. In that year another Act (3 Will. IV.) was passed, which provided for a special "legal" member of Council, not a member of the Company's service, or one of the Executive Council, to sit and vote at all meetings for making laws and regulations. This, in fact, provided for a distinct Legislative Council, apart and separate from the ordinary meetings of the Executive Council. The first additional, or special, member thus appointed, and sent out to India in 1834, was the celebrated historian

Macaulay, and the work to which he gave his powerful aid has been ever since unceasingly carried on. It was, however, too much to expect that one Council sitting in Calcutta could adequately deal with a task so great as the preparation of a code of laws suitable to the customs and circumstances of the varied population of India. Progress was impeded by the necessity of constant references to the subordinate Governments, and the consideration of their demands and suggestions. When, therefore, the government of India passed from the East India Company to the British nation, the opportunity was taken for a fresh departure in the work of legislation, and it was decided to empower the subordinate, or Provincial, Governments to frame and pass all minor Acts required for the administration of their local affairs, leaving the Supreme Council to supervise their work and to frame and pass all measures of Imperial importance, applicable to the Empire generally. This was the origin of the several Supreme and Provincial Legislative Councils, the constitution of which has been already described (see p. 9, *et seq.*).

A special feature in this new arrangement was the admission of a comparatively large number of non-official or independent members, whose local, or special, knowledge might be of service in advising the Government on matters of custom, or on special requirements of the people whose interests they were supposed to represent. No doubt this was a step in a right direction, and it is to be hoped that in time the principle so introduced will be extended, and the constitution of these Councils made more distinctly representative. At present the nominations of non-official members rest with the Governors of the Presidencies; and the necessity of securing a Government majority, which must be observed until the masses of the populace attain a higher standard of political education, forbids any immediate recourse to the system of election by the popular vote.

Great progress has been made during the last twenty years in the work of legislation, and the Indian Statute Book is now in a very satisfactory state of efficiency. Very many of the Acts which have been framed and passed would have little interest for European readers. They provide for the ordinary routine work of Imperial and Provincial administration, such as the levy of customs, excise, opium, salt, and stamp duties, the regulation of police and municipal matters, and numerous similar subjects, down to the control of hackney carriages—all, if not interesting to foreigners, at least very useful in promoting among the people a general sense of government on fixed principles, which each citizen can study for himself and thus place himself beyond reach of extortions formerly practised by unscrupulous office subordinates.

Among measures of Imperial and universal interest, the following Acts may be specially noticed:—

The "Indian Penal Code," which is the statute applicable in all ordinary criminal cases. It contains some provisions not to be found in the corresponding English statutes; for example, adultery is ranked as a criminal offence, and made punishable with imprisonment for any term not exceeding five years.

The code of "Civil Procedure," which provides for the settlement of all civil disputes and similar matters.

The "Indian Succession Act," which codifies the customs of inheritance among Hindoo and Mahometan families, and among Europeans who may have, or who have not, acquired an Indian domicile.

The "Negotiable Instruments Act," a statute of much importance to the trading communities.

The Act for "Registration of Assurances," which provides for the record of all deeds creating any interest or title in landed property —a most valuable statute, the merits of which, and of the Government organization for carrying out its provisions, are thoroughly appreciated by the native community.

The "Joint Stock Companies Act," which much resembles the English statute of similar title and purpose, and is a very valuable piece of legislation for a country like India, where the majority of industrial undertakings can only be worked by associated capital.

Acts providing for the appointments of "Administrators-General" and "Official Assignees," and for the proper discharge of their duties.

INDIAN ARMY.

UNDER the East India Company a large force of both native and European troops was maintained; the latter being raised specially for service in India, and not forming any part of the regular army of Great Britain. The service was popular, and no difficulty was ever experienced in obtaining a superior class of recruit for the Company's European military service. The term of enlistment prior to 1847 was seventeen years, at the end of which time a man could claim his discharge, or could re-enlist, if physically fit, for a further period of five years, receiving a bounty of fifty rupees. After 1847, the Infantry were enlisted for ten years, and the Cavalry and Artillery for twelve years, with option of re-enlisting, if fit, for twelve years more. This arrangement gave the Company a fine body of seasoned European soldiers, whose excellence as fighting material was proved in many a hard-fought battle, and especially during the sepoy mutiny. When the East India Company was abolished and India taken over by the Crown, the Europeans of the Company's local forces were held to be released from their contracts of service; but many re-enlisted under the Queen's colours, and were formed into the new line regiments, the 101st to 109th.

There is no longer any European force raised for service specially in India, but a large proportion of the regular army of Great Britain is permanently on service in India. There is a too general opinion in England that troops are maintained for Indian service at the cost of the British taxpayer, but this is entirely a false impression. India pays for every man whose services she obtains, and probably for a good many from whom she gets very little service. Every item of expense connected with the recruiting for regiments on the Indian establishment, transport between India and England, etc., is charged to her; and under the present short-service system there can be no doubt that she has to pay for the transport of many whose service with the colours in India is of most limited duration. Practically, India relieves the British taxpayer of the expenses of one-third of the regular army of Great Britain, and at a price which most probably far exceeds the cost at which a similar number of men could be maintained for local service exclusively, on a system of enlistment for a long term of years, such as was in force under the East India Company.

The average strength of the Indian army may be taken to be 180,000 (exclusive of officers), of which 60,000 are European troops belonging to the army of Great Britain, but placed at the disposal of the Indian Government in the absence of demand for their services elsewhere, and 120,000 are native troops.

The distribution of this force, including officers serving with the colours, is much as follows:—

EUROPEAN TROOPS.

	Commissioned officers.		Non-commissioned officers and privates.
Bengal	2592	......	37,745
Madras	974	......	11,413
Bombay	848	......	10,937
	4414		60,095

NATIVE TROOPS.

	Officers. European.	Officers. Native.		Non-commissioned officers and privates.
Bengal	749	1453	......	62,929
Madras	372	709	......	33,130
Bombay	315	590	......	25,636
	1436	2752		121,695
	4188			

It will doubtless be remarked that the number of officers belonging to the native army is considerably smaller than that allotted to the European troops (although the native is nearly twice the size of the European force), the discrepancy being specially noticeable in the number of European officers. Many are of opinion that, with the general use of arms of precision, the proportion of European officers with native troops is too small, and might cause serious embarrassment on active service.

The annual cost of this force is close upon sixteen millions sterling, of which about twelve millions is spent in India, and nearly four millions in England. The Indian Government accounts do not distinguish between the total cost of the European and that of the native troops, except in a very few items, and without full particulars it is impossible to draw a comparison between the cost of the two forces. But there can be no doubt that the cost of the European troops, exclusive of mere pay and allowances, is very heavy, and where any separate particulars of the expenditure in India are given by the Government accounts, it would appear, in spite of the great difference in numbers, to equal, and sometimes to exceed, that of the native troops. The home charges, amounting to nearly four millions annually, would seem to be almost exclusively due to the European force, and the cost of transport, some £500,000 annually, is also clearly chargeable to that head.

The Indian army is primarily under the "Horse Guards," the chief or central control being exercised in England, and all the main administrative appointments made by the Crown. There is a Commander-in-Chief of India, who holds office for five years, and, under orders from England, supervises the military affairs of the Empire. The Madras and Bombay armies have each separate Commanders-in-Chief, with respective head-quarters staff; and the usual divisional commands are entrusted to generals appointed by the Horse Guards. There seems to be little good object in the maintenance of these separate establishments for the minor Presidencies. While the railway and telegraph system was still incomplete, independent armies, each complete in all details, were essential to safety. But recent years have brought great changes, not only in the rapidity of intercommunication, but also in the strength and composition of the provincial native forces; and it seems probable that the entire Indian army might now be safely placed under the control of one Commander-in-Chief for the whole of India.

Heavy ordnance, shot and shell, and small-arms are still supplied to the Indian army from England; but gunpowder, cartridges, bullets, clothing, and many similar necessaries, are locally manufactured at various Government factories The tendency is towards "centralization" of such factories in Bengal and Northern India; but discussion on the merits or dangers of this principle hardly comes within the scope of this treatise.

India is largely dependent upon Australia for horses for European Cavalry and Artillery. The Government has "stud" or breeding establishments in Northern India, but the number of horses obtainable there can only meet a small part of the requirements, and without the Australian supply there would be serious difficulty in keeping the mounted forces in state for efficient service.

POLICE.

When the East India Company began to undertake the administration of its provinces, the police system of the country was practically confined to an establishment of watchmen, provided and paid for by such communities or individuals as required or could afford the protection of their property. This state of matters was gradually improved, but it was not until some twenty years ago that any systematic organization of police became general throughout the country. The system now in force is based upon that of Great Britain. Each Presidency town has its separate establishment, while the country towns and districts are under charge of a district police, similar to our system of a county constabulary. The force is placed under the control of Inspectors-General in all the main divisions of the Empire. These are usually military officers of high position. The more strictly departmental work is entrusted to District Superintendents and their assistants, each of whom supervises a very considerable district. They are largely drawn from the Army Staff Corps at present, but as promotion takes place these appointments will probably be more filled by men who have been specially trained in the lower grades of the police service—Europeans, East Indians, and natives. The subdivisions of the force are under inspectors and sub-inspectors, many of them Europeans of good position and education; while the rank and file is, of course, chiefly composed of native head constables and constables.

The total force of the Empire may be taken to average as follows:—

260 district superintendents and their assistants;
1050 inspectors;
2250 sub-inspectors;
14,000 head constables;
90,000 constables—

under the charge of six Inspectors-General and twelve Assistant Inspectors-General. In addition to the above regular force, there is a considerable establishment of village watchmen, known as chowkeedars and talliaries. The annual cost of the police establishment of the Empire averages some £2,300,000.

The Government of India has for some time asserted the principle that police protection of property and person should not be a charge on Imperial funds; but that each community, or province, or district should support the burden of its own police establishment, the State contributing in each instance a fair proportion of the annual charge in return for the services of the police in watching Government property, furnishing guards for treasuries, escorts for treasure-parties while transporting treasure from the interior to central or Presidency treasuries, and similar duties. This principle has already been introduced in the cities of Bombay and Calcutta, where the maintenance of the town police has been accepted by those municipalities; but in Madras the town has not, as yet, been able to afford the required contribution. Efforts will, no doubt, be made to extend the application of the principle, but great opposition must be expected in the rural districts. It must be remembered that the bulk of the population of India is agricultural, and that the land is held from the State, as explained in the chapter on Land Revenue, on a system of an annual payment, or land tax, or assessment, the origin of which was the cession by the cultivator to the landlord of a certain proportion of the produce of the soil. It is contended by the cultivators that, according to immemorial usage, the landlord is bound, in return for such payment, to secure the cultivator in the quiet and secure enjoyment of his property; and it is urged that the imposition of a separate cess to cover police charges would be a violation of this contract; that police protection is already paid for in the assessment on land, and therefore should be defrayed from those Imperial resources to which the revenue from land so largely contributes.

The district police are to some extent instructed in military drill, and are armed with rifles and trained in their use, thus forming a valuable auxiliary to regular troops in case of need, and capable of being employed efficiently in putting down any minor disturbance or insubordination to Government orders. It seems probable that, in course of time, a judicious increase in the police establishment may enable considerable reductions to be made in the present military expenditure of the Empire.

MEDICAL.

It would be difficult to exaggerate the importance to the Empire of the medical establishment maintained by the Government of India. For, with the exception of one or two isolated instances in the large Presidency towns, and a few doctors specially retained and supported by the planters in the large tea, coffee, and indigo districts, there are no private European practitioners in the country; while the native so-called doctors, not in the Government service, are practically devoid of any special training or knowledge. The entire medical charge of the European and Native civil population, including such details as sanitation, vaccination, the charge of hospitals and dispensaries, lunatic asylums, and the education in medical colleges and schools, necessarily devolves upon the Government Civil Medical Establishment. The army is separately provided for. British troops are under the special care of the British Army Medical Staff, the members of which take their regular turn of foreign service in India, and are not employed in civil duties; but the native troops are, as a general rule, under the charge of the Indian medical establishment. The expenditure on medical services rendered to the army is included in the general return of military charges, and forms no part of the annual return of the cost of the Indian civil medical establishment.

The annual charge for medical services in the civil department averages £650,000, and may be analyzed as follows:—

On hospitals and dispensaries	£216,000
Vaccination	67,000
Lunatic asylums	50,000
Medical colleges and schools	45,000
General	272,000
	£650,000

With the exception of a few institutions specially endowed by wealthy and patriotic natives, all the hospitals, dispensaries, and asylums in British India have been provided and are maintained by the Government. The public hospitals, so common in Europe, supported by charitable contributions aud subscriptions, and the similar institutions for the blind, deaf, and dumb, etc., etc., are practically unknown in India. The State has had, as a general rule, to provide for everything connected with the medical treatment of the population.

The medical establishment, as it now exists, is a singular instance of the vitality of old institutions. It originated with the staff attached by the old East India Company to its military establishment; and though at present the great proportion of its members are employed in duties of a purely civil character, all of them are still ranked as Military surgeons, wear uniform, and are under the orders of the Commander-in-Chief of their respective Presidencies. It is difficult to see what good object can be gained by the perpetuation of a system belonging to conditions of Indian government which have long since passed away; or why the present Indian Medical Department should not be treated as, what it is in fact, a purely civil administration.

Every principal station, or seat of Government offices in the different districts, is provided with a medical officer of the military rank of surgeon or assistant-surgeon, with a dispensary and a sufficient staff of dispensers and assistants, and wherever the population is of any importance with a hospital also. The services of this establishment are available gratis to all, natives or Europeans, who may attend at the dispensary or hospital for advice or treatment. The medical officer has further to attend to all servants on the Government establishment; to the inmates of all jails, etc., in his district; and to all matters concerning sanitation and vaccination. He is free to attend non-official Europeans or natives at their residences, on the usual fees charged by physicians in England, and in the large towns this privilege of private practice adds considerably to the income of doctors of experience and established reputation. It should also be added that, but for this concession by Government, the large class of non-officials, traders, and professional men now resident in India, together with their families, would find great difficulty (if not an absolute impossibility) in getting skilled medical assistance when required.

It will be seen that members of this service have plenty to do; and it may be imagined that in seasons of calamity, such as a severe outbreak of cholera, or periods of dearth or famine, their position is by no means an enviable one. Every man who has lived in India can testify to the zeal and self-devotion displayed at all times, and especially on occasions of emergency, by the Indian medical officers.

The Government of India has established medical colleges in its principal towns, where diplomas are granted to students of proved proficiency in surgery and medicine. Considerable numbers of natives and East Indians are trained in these establishments, and pass into Government employment in the district dispensaries and hospitals; and in time many of the higher appointments will, no doubt, be occupied by natives of the country, so trained. Of late years also, several classes for the instruction of women have been instituted; and in the Presidency towns there are several ladies who have received their diplomas and are now practising, mainly among the native female community. It is very desirable that this movement should be supported and encouraged, for native customs are opposed to the treatment of respectable females by male doctors, and an immense amount of bad health and mortality among the better class of native women is entirely due to the want of good medical advice and treatment. In fact, it cannot be doubted that there is a great field in India for the lucrative practice of medicine by skilled European lady doctors among the respectable native female community.

EDUCATION.

THE Government of India has for a long time given much attention to the education of the people, and it may be affirmed that in no country of the world are such facilities for the attainment of knowledge provided for the masses of the population, at such small expense to those immediately benefited. In proof of this, it may be stated that the annual gross expenditure of the State under this head averages over one million sterling, while the receipts from school fees, sale of books, etc., only reach about £100,000, or only one-tenth of the expenses, leaving a net annual charge on the revenue of the Empire of some £900,000, as the cost of the education provided for the youth of the country.

There is no attempt at compulsory education, nor is this needed, for the people are only too ready to avail themselves of the means for knowledge brought so largely within their reach, even in the remotest villages. The paternal care of the Government has covered the country with a network of village, primary, normal, low, middle, and high schools, besides colleges in the Presidency and other large towns, and many special training schools for those who wish to study engineering, medicine, law, industries, etc.; and these are available for students on a scale of fees so low as to be almost nominal. It would be too lengthy, and almost impossible, to give accurately detailed statistics of the number, position, etc., of all these establishments. It will be sufficient to say that this great scheme of work is supervised by 10 Inspectors-General or

Directors of Public Instruction; by over 450 inspectors, sub-inspectors, and deputies; and by nearly 5500 principals, professors, head-masters, masters, and teachers of all grades. The higher appointments are usually filled by Europeans, many of them of distinguished ability and attainments; and the service offers considerable inducements in emoluments and position, which should always secure for it a high class of office-holders.

The Government high schools and colleges have turned out many men of whose proved abilities and career India may well be proud; while undoubtedly a very large number, of possibly not inferior capacity and attainments, have not yet had the opportunity of turning their knowledge to practical account for the benefit of their country.

It is often said that the Government should confine its assistance to the provision of a plain elementary education to the masses, and that it is not the duty of a State to provide, at great cost to the public, an expensive University education to all comers, the majority of whom cannot possibly find opportunity for turning such a high standard of acquirements to practical account, while they are, in fact, morally unfitted by it for the ordinary avocations of the class in life to which they belong. There can be no doubt that these higher schools and colleges are annually turning out a large body of young men who cannot find employment in the various offices or departments of the Government, or in private offices (the supply of candidates for such work being enormously in excess of the demand), and who are practically unsuited for, as they are unwilling to undertake, work of any other character. And it is feared the presence of a large body of intelligent, well-educated, unemployed, and needy men, widely scattered throughout the country, must carry with it some elements of possible mischief. In connection with this, the necessity for stringent measures to repress the growing audacity and licence of writers in the vernacular newspapers, as shown by the introduction by the Government of the "Vernacular Press Act," is of considerable significance.

ECCLESIASTICAL.

THE Indian Empire maintains a considerable establishment for the spiritual wants of those of its servants who profess the Christian faith, and the services of this establishment are extended to non-official Europeans and other Christians resident within the Empire. The average strength of this establishment may be stated as follows:—4 bishops (of whom one is the Roman Catholic Bishop of Bombay); 3 archdeacons; 180 chaplains, besides various registrars, clerks, and other minor functionaries.

The Bishop of Calcutta is the metropolitan or head; Madras and Bombay have each a bishop. Of the 180 chaplains, the majority are Church of England, but a few of the Church of Scotland are included.

The annual charge on revenues for the maintenance of this establishment is about £164,000, and is a subject of much complaint among the educated natives of the country. These allege, and no doubt with truth, that of all the religious bodies in the Empire, the Christian alone, or, more strictly, the Church of England, is permitted to be a burden upon the public exchequer. All other sections of the community provide, at their own expense, buildings and men for their religious services. It must be admitted that there is some ground for the complaint; for, although it may be argued that those servants of the State whom it is necessary for the common advantage to import are entitled to provision for their spiritual wants, and such provision is a part of the price the Empire must pay for their services, no such plea can be urged in respect of the large number of non-official Europeans who have selected India as a seat of labour for a livelihood, and these latter should provide, at their own expense, for their own spiritual wants, as for their temporal. Moreover, the support of the Government is chiefly confined to the Church of England. There are large numbers of clergy in India, mainly employed in missionary work, belonging to the Roman Catholic Church and to various "dissenting" bodies, who are supported entirely by subscriptions from Europe and America, and who minister very largely to the spiritual needs of native and East Indian Christians, and to many of the class of European non-officials. This question of State support to one special Church establishment deserves more attention than it has yet received.

RAILWAYS.

The construction of railways in India commenced in 1849. No one acquainted with the country could fail to see the urgent necessity for a system of railways, not only in the interests of trade and the development of the internal resources of the country, but also from a strategical or political standpoint. But it seemed unlikely that funds for this purpose could be got from a population totally unacquainted with the nature and advantages of a railway system; while foreign capitalists not unnaturally felt uncertain as to the cost of construction and working, and the probable traffic returns, in a country still so unsettled, and where the extent of the internal trade was yet, to a great degree, unknown. The Government, recognizing the great addition to the practical strength of its military establishments which would be gained by the power of rapid communication and transport, resolved to guarantee a minimum revenue or interest on all capital subscribed, and with this guarantee the funds required were readily obtained in England. Since 1849, eight main lines have been completed, viz.—

The East Indian Railway;
Great Indian Peninsula Railway;
Madras Railway;
Bombay, Baroda, and Central India;
Sind, Punjaub, and Delhi;
Oudh and Rohilkund;
Eastern Bengal;
South Indian.

These have a total aggregate length of 6044

miles, of which 805 miles are laid with a double line of metals, and the balance is worked on a single line. Of recent years the Indian Government has adopted the plan of constructing all minor lines of railways as "State railways," or as part of the "Productive Public Works" of the Empire; the cost of construction being provided out of the current annual revenues. There are twenty-seven such lines completed and in construction, and four other projects are under survey. The completed portion contains 2171 miles of line, and there are still about 1000 miles of sanctioned projects to finish.

The extent, therefore, of completed railway lines, "guaranteed" and "State," is 8215 miles. This work has been done for a total expenditure of £118,016,755, say.

Guaranteed	£96,725,679
State	21,291,076

It may be added that, out of a total of 64,321 registered holders of Indian railway shares or stock, only 317 are natives of India. From this it may be seen how impossible it would be to raise money by local subscription for an Indian railway system; and the expediency of the plan now adopted, under which the funds required are practically raised by the yearly taxation of the population, becomes obvious.

Of the guaranteed lines, the East Indian, Great Indian Peninsula, and Eastern Bengal are the only ones which appear to give a net revenue in excess of the guaranteed interest. The other five do not earn sufficient to cover the amount guaranteed. On the aggregate, however, the net earnings of the eight lines appear to leave a surplus of about £290,000 over the guaranteed interest; the figures being—

Net revenue	£5,002,028
Minimum guaranteed interest ...	4,708,134

The State railways appear to give a net return of only £195,787, or something under one per cent. on capital expended; but many of these lines are still incomplete, and only partially opened for traffic, and there can be no doubt that in time the returns will greatly increase.

Recent official returns give the following statistics of annual receipts from passengers and goods on all the lines:—

Passengers	£2,844,508
Goods	6,365,599
Gross receipts	9,200,107
Total working expenses	4,178,582
	£5,021,525

The passenger traffic, again, is analyzed as follows:—

GUARANTEED LINES.

First class passengers	192,257
Second ditto, ditto	791,901
Third and fourth ditto, ditto	31,216,255
	32,200,413

STATE.

First class passengers	25,285
Second ditto, ditto	159,729
Third and fourth ditto, ditto	6,104,159
	6,289,173
Total on guaranteed and State railways	38,489,586

The enormous difference between the number of first and second class and the aggregate of third and fourth class passengers will at once arrest attention. It shows conclusively that India requires a cheap system of railway communication, more than the luxurious conveniences of Western countries.

Another striking peculiarity of Indian railways, as compared with those of Europe, is the small amount of "mineral" traffic as compared with goods, as shown by the following figures:—

GUARANTEED LINES.

	Tons.
Minerals	788,539
Goods	6,341,056

STATE RAILWAYS.

Minerals	50,133
Goods	955,279

TOTAL GUARANTEED AND STATE.

	Tons.
Minerals	838,672
Goods	7,296,335

But of this "mineral" traffic, nearly the whole is coal and coke for the use of the locomotive department, and not on account of the public customers, or traffic producing a revenue.

It will be observed that, under this system of State railway construction, the Empire is gradually acquiring a property which should in time become a valuable source of revenue. These State railway lines are, in fact, actual investments of capital, and may be taken in the annual balance sheet as assets of the State, exactly in the same way as a manufacturer may put down his mill or foundry as property unrealized, but realizable in case of need to pay liabilities. Looking at foregoing figures, it will be seen that the Indian Government have expended out of current revenues over twenty-one millions on the construction of State lines; and it may be assumed, therefore, that the Empire possesses in this particular an unrealized asset of twenty-one millions sterling to set in part against a funded debt of one hundred and fifty-six millions; or, in other words, that India possesses property in "State railways" sufficient to pay fourteen per cent. of its national debt. In the case of guaranteed railways, the Empire has the option of taking over the lines at any time, on payment of the capital at the average price of the stock during the three preceding years, or on such other terms as may be mutually agreed upon. It has already exercised this privilege in the case of the East Indian Railway, having acquired that property by purchase from the proprietors on the basis of an annuity to the late shareholders of £5 12*s.* 6*d.* per cent. of capital, to continue until 1953, when the line will become the unencumbered property of the Empire. It is estimated that during the currency of this contract for purchase, calculating the net traffic earnings at only the present annual average of £2,495,000, the State will realize a surplus equal to £337,892 per annum, against £165,287, which is its present share of surplus net profits after payment of guaranteed interest, or a clear gain of £172,605 per annum over the old arrangement. After 1953 the whole of the net traffic earnings will pass to the State, and the railway will become a valuable source of revenue, providing, at present figures of traffic, nearly one-half of the annual charge for interest on the present national debt of India; while, taken as a realizable asset, the value of the line, some thirty-two millions, will cover twenty per cent. of the capital debt. Taking this thirty-two millions with the present value of State railways, twenty-one millions, we have fifty-three millions of railway property to set against one hundred and fifty-six millions of debt, or fully thirty-four per cent. of the debt secured by this class of property alone. With such figures before us, it seems strange that we should hear, as we have recently heard, statements that India is rapidly becoming bankrupt.

The railways employ on the working lines 142,200 persons, of whom 135,300, or over ninety-five per cent., are natives; 3416, or 2·40 per cent., are East Indians; and 3485, or 2·45 per cent., Europeans. Measures are under consideration for providing special schools at hill sanitaria for the large number of children (over 5000) of the Europeans employed.

In the Appendix will be found a statement of the length of each railway which has been completed or sanctioned or is in course of construction.

POST OFFICE.

THIS department is in India, as in all other countries, under the direct control of the Government; and the work is well organized, ample facilities being supplied even in the remotest districts of the country. On all the railways the mails are carried free of charge, this being one of the conditions on which the Government of India guaranteed the interest on the railway capital. Where there are no railways, the work is done by mail-carts and post-runners, paid by the State. The money order system is in operation throughout the country, and is largely availed of by all classes for the transmission of small sums.

The annual expenditure of the Postal Department averages some £950,000, and the receipts about £870,000, leaving a deficiency, or charge on public revenues, of some £80,000 a year; but the tendency is towards an increase of revenue; and with the rapid progress of education, and improvement in means of communication between the districts, it is probable that before long the department will cease to be a charge upon State funds, and may even become a source of revenue. Hitherto the chief control of the department has generally been entrusted to Postmasters-General selected from the favoured class of covenanted civilians. Whether a more special training and technical knowledge than such gentlemen can have had the opportunity of acquiring would not operate to advantage in the increase of revenue, is a question which deserves and would probably repay further examination.

TELEGRAPHS.

THE Government of India has covered the country with a network of telegraph lines, connecting all the important towns, and stations or seats of Government establishments, and providing for the requirements of commerce or the convenience of individuals. The lines are very largely used in the despatch of the Government work, and certain of the higher State officials have the power to "clear the line," or, in other words, to give precedence to important State messages over all other business. The only private telegraph lines in India are those of the railways, which are mainly used for the working of the roads but are also open to any of the public who may have occasion to telegraph to towns or stations on the railway line. The annual expenditure on the Indian telegraph establishment is about £500,000, and the average receipts about £350,000, leaving a deficiency of some £150,000 as an annual charge on the Imperial revenues. This, of course, should not be the case; and it is probable that careful inspection and enquiry into the working of the department by men who have been accustomed to supervise telegraph establishments in Europe or America would result in advantage to the country. The rates charged for messages are very high—two shillings for every six words (address not counted), and, of course, must check the free use of the wires, and confine it to absolutely indispensable messages. The revenue derivable from the public could probably be very greatly increased by a judicious reduction of charges, and check on unnecessary use of the wires in Government business.

It is worth notice that all this fine property, for such it must be considered, has been gradually created out of the ordinary annual revenues of the Empire. It is another item of State property of very considerable value—in fact, an asset of the Empire, available for the discharge in part of the State liability on the funded debt; and, if properly managed, should pay at least as high a rate of interest on its capital cost as is paid on the Indian debt.

MUNICIPALITIES.

THE Government of India has for some years past promoted the organization of local government among the Urban and large Village Communities, with special reference to the construction and maintenance of roads, general sanitation, and similar matters, which in former years were either undertaken by the Government or altogether neglected.

These municipalities are usually placed under the direction of the chief covenanted civilian of the district, who is *ex-officio* President. In the country districts the members of the Board are appointed by Government, but in the larger Presidency towns one-half of the members are elected by the ratepayers, and the remainder nominated by Government. Such arrangements should always give a Government majority on these Boards; but in addition to this primary influence, the Government exercises a very considerable control over the acts of the municipalities; insists upon needful works of communication, water supply, drainage, etc., being undertaken; and claims an ultimate right to "veto" any orders of the Board providing for taxation, or levy of local cesses or rates, of which it may disapprove. The Government further proposes to place all such matters as police, hospitals, and education, within the limits of a municipality under the special charge of the town, and at the special cost of the inhabitants, instead of, as at present, under the control of Government and at the charge of Imperial funds. This measure will, no doubt, excite much opposition, and it may be doubted whether the populations of Indian towns and villages can at present afford such heavy burdens.

The number of municipalities at present in India is about 800, divided as follows :—

Bengal	194
Punjaub	199
North-West Provinces	80
Oudh	24
British Burmah	7
Central Provinces	57
Bombay	194
Madras	48

But this number will, no doubt, be rapidly increased. The main difficulty is in getting the natives to take an intelligent interest in the improvements of their towns or villages, and to overcome their dislike to any changes of old custom, and to any outlay of money on sanitary objects of which they do not appreciate the advantages.

PAUPERISM.

THERE is no State arrangement for the relief of the native poor in India, but there are numerous almshouses, supported by endowments from charitable natives and others, where relief is given to those in want. Many of the large temples also apply a portion of their income to similar purposes. Natives, as a general rule, support the aged and infirm members of their family; and almsgiving is a religious duty with Hindoos and Mahometans alike. All these causes combine to prevent any necessity for State interference, except on occasions of general scarcity or famine.

In the case of destitute Europeans, an Act of the legislature, known as "The Vagrant Act," empowers the police to arrest any European wandering about the country in destitution, or without visible means of subsistence. Or any such European may go to the nearest police station and declare himself to be a "vagrant." In such cases the sufferer is forwarded, under police supervision, to the nearest Presidency town, where he is lodged and fed in an establishment provided by the Government for this purpose, for a reasonable interval, while attempts are made to find suitable employment for him. Should this not be procurable, he is "deported," or sent out of the country, at Government expense, to England, or Australia, or elsewhere he may reasonably desire. In this manner the scandal, and possible danger to public security, of Europeans without employment wandering about the country in a state of destitution, and sometimes intimidating and ill-using the natives, is avoided.

LAND REVENUE.

THE "sheet anchor" of Indian finance is the tax on cultivated land, known as "land revenue." To trace the actual origin of this tax and the various systems under which it has been levied in different parts of the country by different rulers in past ages, its actual incidence on different forms of cultivation, its economical effects, etc., etc., would require a volume, and it is impossible to give in these pages more than a brief outline of the institution. So far as can be ascertained, the principle of tenure, or proprietary right in land, recognized by all Hindoo communities from the most remote ages was this—that the man who first cleared and cultivated waste land (and all land must have been originally waste) acquired a perpetual right of occupancy of such land, subject only to the payment to his sovereign, or feudal superior, of a share of the produce of the soil. There is much controversy as to the actual nature of this right of occupancy; whether, for example, it amounts to an actual ownership of the land, with all manorial privileges, or whether it is only of the nature of a perpetual lease. It is, however indisputable that whatever the exact legal tenure may have been, it has always been treated as an alienable possession—a right which the occupying cultivator could mortgage or sell, and which descended to his heirs in perpetuity so long as the "Crown dues" were regularly paid; but which, in default of such payment, could be attached and sold by "the Crown," whose claim moreover took precedence of all other creditors, or holders of "encumbrances." This was the system which the East India Company found in force upon the territories ceded to, or conquered by, it. The officers of the Company, whose experience was limited to the counting-houses of the trading factories, were, as a rule, very imperfectly acquainted with the conditions of village life and agriculture in the interior, and quite incompetent to enter into yearly settlements with each individual cultivator (many with holdings of only two or three acres) over a vast extent of country. But the chief advantage derivable from the acquired territories lay in the rents, or dues, payable by the cultivators, and it was necessary to provide some system of revenue collection. In Northern India the territory first acquired—Bengal, Behar, and Orissa—was handed over to middle men, or Zemindars, who took up large tracts, or estates, from the Company on permanent leases, at a fixed rental—themselves collecting from the cultivator the dues payable to the Crown. It is pretty certain that a considerable margin of profit remains with the zemindar under such an arrangement. In Southern India the Company's servants, under the able management of Sir T. Munro, were able to continue the native system of direct dealings with each cultivator on yearly agreements; and this is still the form of settlement over the greater portion of the Madras Presidency. There have been various changes or "settlements" introduced during the present century, and several different systems of fixed rentals for certain terms of years are in existence; but the main principle which underlies the whole is—that the occupying cultivator cannot be ousted from his holding so long as he pays the fixed assessment. No matter whether the settlement is direct between cultivator and Government, or made through a zemindar or middle man to the Government, or through a village community to the Government, the principle is the same, viz. that the State receives a share of the produce of all cultivated land in recognition of its sovereign rights, and in consideration of protection to the cultivator from invasion or internal disturbance. This share of the produce of the land was originally, under the native sovereigns, collected "in kind," but has long since been commuted into a money payment. What was the proportion of produce taken by the native rulers is doubtful; it probably depended a good deal on circumstances. Native tradition fixes it at one-half, but considers the cultivator seldom managed to retain more than one quarter. The present money assessment is believed to represent about one-fourth of the produce; but authorities disagree greatly on this subject, and the most difficult questions which the Government settlement officers have had to solve have been—the yield per acre of different kinds of produce on different soils, and the average market values of such produce. Bearing in mind how greatly such value at the place of production must be affected by the existence, or the absence, of lines of easy communication with the coast or large interior markets, it is easy to understand that the value of lands of equal powers of production may vary considerably in different parts of the same district. It is to be feared that the Indian Government has not yet succeeded in introducing uniformly equitable rates of assessment in the different districts of the country; and though undoubtedly the great progress which has been made of recent years in opening up the interior by roads and railways is tending to the advantage of the cultivators as a body, yet there is room for the belief that the great difference which is observable in different parts of India in the social condition and prosperity of the inhabitants, may be due to the unequal incidence of the Government assessment, calculated on the assumed market value of the land's produce, upon tracts of land of probably equal productive powers.

The total collection of land revenue in British India averages twenty-two millions sterling, distributed as follows :—

Bengal	£3,696,210
North-West Provinces and Oudh ...	5,346,759
Punjaub	1,933,174
British Burmah	785,648
Assam	362,972
Central Provinces	601,955
	£12,726,718
Madras	4,494,888
Bombay	3,662,346
Territories under the Government of India	82,088
The Berars	616,348
	£21,582,388

It will be seen that, taking the main divisions of population, the incidence of land revenue taxation is about as follows :—

Bengal, including North-West Provinces, Oudh, Punjaub, etc., with 137,388,916 of population, gives a total land revenue of £12,726,718, or about 1*s*. 10*d*. per head, or £20 19*s*. 2*d*. per square mile, or 8*d*. per acre (cultivated and waste alike).

Madras, with 31,281,177 of population, gives £4,494,888 of revenue, or about 2*s*. 10½*d*. per head, or £32 10*s*. 9*d*. per square mile, or over 1*s*. per acre (cultivated and waste).

Bombay, with a population of 16,228,774, gives revenue £3,662,346 ; say 4*s*. 6½*d*. per head, or £29 8*s*. 6*d*. per square mile, or 11*d*. per acre (cultivated and waste).

In this calculation Bengal is taken to include various provinces besides Bengal proper—a somewhat misleading estimate if we wish to compare Bengal with the other chief Presidencies; as a matter of fact Bengal proper with a population of 62,724,840 gives only £3,696,210 of land revenue, or less than 1*s*. 2*d*. per head, as against 2*s*. 10½*d*. per head in Madras, and 4*s*. 6½*d*. per head in Bombay. This is worthy of notice. Bengal proper is almost entirely under zemindary settlement. Its soil is notoriously the most fertile of India, and it is impossible to suppose that, if the Government share of produce in the less favoured districts of Madras and Bombay is worth the figures realized in those provinces, the due proportion of produce is paid to the State in Bengal. There is another point of view of considerable importance as affecting the social condition of the people. It has been much disputed whether the undoubtedly impoverished condition of the average Indian cultivator is not caused by a heavier demand for land-tax than his land can fairly pay. It is worthy of remark that, as shown by above figures, the most prosperous province, *Bengal*, appears to be the one most lightly assessed. *Madras*, which pays a much heavier assessment, is notoriously a poor and backward Presidency; while in *Bombay*, which is the most heavily assessed of all, the state of the cultivators has become so desperate that a special Act of the legislature for their relief from the extortions of village money-lenders is now under trial.

The objection may certainly be raised that comparison should properly be made on the actual revenue from the several *cultivated* areas; but it is difficult to get accurate returns of area permanently under cultivation, and in a country like India, where the great majority of the people are cultivators of small holdings, we may fairly base inquiry on the incidence per head of the taxation on cultivation.

OPIUM.

THE Government of India derives a large annual revenue from the manufacture and sale of this drug; a monopoly of the old East India Company, which has not yet been abandoned.

In British India the manufacture is restricted to two agencies in Behar and Benares, under the administration of the Government of Bengal, and under the direct supervision of a special

Opium Department. The cultivation and manufacture is carried on by the ordinary ryots or landholders; no compulsion is exercised, and it is optional with any ryot to cultivate or not. Those who wish to cultivate in any year enter into engagements for the season with the agents of the Opium Department, and receive advances of money. The cultivation begins in the autumn, and the drug is manufactured and ready for delivery by the following July. The ryots are paid at a fixed price—5*s.* per lb.—delivered of a standard consistency.

The opium so procured is divided into "abkaree," or "excise" opium, for consumption in the country through licensed shops; and "provision" opium, for exportation only. The latter description is sent down to Calcutta, where it is sold by auction to the highest bidders in a series of sales.

About 500,000 acres are ordinarily cultivated in this manner, under the supervision of the Opium Department, and from 45,000 to 55,000 chests, each containing about 130 lbs. net weight of opium, are manufactured. This would give a return of about 12 lbs. of opium per acre. About 4000 chests are retained for home consumption, and the remainder is sold in Calcutta for export. It may be calculated that the drug costs about

7*s.* per lb., and is sold at about 18*s.* to 20*s.* The annual cost of manufacture to Government, including establishment, may be taken to average two to two and a quarter millions, and the receipts five to six millions sterling; the net revenue averaging from three to three and three quarter millions sterling, though in some years these figures are considerably exceeded. For several years past, owing to larger production and higher prices, the net receipts have been from one and a half to two millions above these figures. A considerable quantity of opium is also produced in the independent territory of Malwa (Central India), which is permitted to pass through British India for exportation, but for no other purpose, and on payment of a transit duty of Rs. 600 per chest (or about 9*s.* per lb.) as it passes the frontier. Over 40,000 chests are thus passed annually, and the Government receives a transit duty of about two and a half millions sterling from this source alone.

The net revenue, therefore, from profits on manufacture of Bengal opium and transit duties on Malwa opium may be estimated to average from five and a half to six millions sterling, which in exceptional years may rise to as much as eight millions. But this opium revenue is notoriously subject to fluctuations; and it is seldom that the Finance Minister's estimates are not widely different from results. It may be seriously questioned whether it would not be an advantage to abolish the monopoly, and throw the cultivation and manufacture open in certain districts, merely charging an excise duty. Under the present system, the cost of manufacture, including the establishment, approaches half the saleable value of the drug, and an excise duty of Rs. 600 to Rs. 700 per chest would probably give as large a revenue as is now derived from the monopoly with all its elaborate and costly administrative machinery. The transit duty on Malwa opium is collected at a charge of about one-eighth per cent. on the realized revenue; the charges being about £3000 on a revenue of two and a half millions. It might fairly be expected in this instance, as in most others, that private enterprise would increase and cheapen production, and that an excise duty would give Government a larger revenue, with infinitely less labour and expense in administrative machinery than is at present incurred.

SALT.

THE Government of India derives a considerable revenue through a duty on this article. The average returns are as follows :—

Gross receipts	...	...	...	£7,335,000
Less charges	...	...	...	356,000
Net revenue	...	...	...	£6,979,000

The supply is largely from the sea-coast, where it is manufactured, under Government supervision, by the simple process of evaporating sea water in shallow pans or beds. A further large quantity is imported from Europe, chiefly Cheshire salt; the balance is obtained from various salt mines and lakes in the Punjaub and North-West Provinces. It may be roughly estimated that, of the total consumption, 50 per cent. is coast manufacture, 25 per cent. from inland works, and 25 per cent. imported European salt. A tax on salt has always been a main source of revenue in India. The British, on their first admission into the country, found the Mahometan rulers collecting imposts on the manufacture, and transport duties on the conveyance from places of production into the interior. The East India Company soon turned the custom of the country to account, and various systems were one after another introduced, of monopolies and farming licenses to private individuals, and ultimately of manufacture and sale under direct Government supervision. The general principle of this latter arrangement is—that the salt is made by private enterprise and risk, at certain specified places, under Government control, and delivered to the Government officials at a fixed price. It is then stored at convenient central depôts, for disposal to wholesale merchants at its cost plus the Government duty. The rate of duty has been considerably altered from time to time, and has not been uniform in different districts, varying until lately from Rs. 3-4*as.* (6*s.* 6*d.*) to Rs. 1-13*as.* (3*s.* 7½*d.*) per maund (82 lbs.). It has now, however, been consolidated into a uniform rate of Rs. 2-8*as.* (5*s.*) for the bulk of British India ; but in Bengal, where large quantities of foreign salt are imported, it has been fixed at Rs. 2-14*as.* (5*s.* 9*d.*) It is difficult to frame accurate estimates of the consumption, as many native chiefs are allowed certain privileges of obtaining an annual supply free, or at reduced rates of duty, and there is little doubt that in many parts of India a considerable amount of secret or illicit manufacture is carried on. The Government returns of consumption in British India also include a considerable quantity of salt which pays duty but is passed into native territory, and it is, therefore, difficult to know over what figures of population the consumption should be spread. If we accept the Government returns of about twenty-eight millions of maunds as the annual consumption in British India, exclusive of British Burmah, or say one hundred and eighty-two millions of inhabitants, we have a consumption per head of 11 lbs. per annum; but, for the reasons above stated, it is probable that the consumption is spread over a larger population than that of British India, and the average quantity consumed per head is therefore somewhat smaller than the above estimate.

EXCISE.

THE Indian Government charge an excise duty on country-manufactured spirits, on opium consumed in the country, and on certain intoxicating drugs. The revenue averages two and a half millions sterling, or about 3¼*d.* per head; of which one and three quarter million is derived from spirits, about £500,000 from opium, and £250,000 from drugs. The collections vary considerably in the different districts. In regard to spirits, for example, Madras gives about £700,000, or $5\frac{1}{2}$*d.* per head of its population; and Bombay about £350,000, or $5\frac{1}{4}$*d.* per head. Bengal proper gives £425,000, or nearly $1\frac{1}{2}$*d.* per head; while Oudh, the Punjaub, and North-West Provinces give only £250,000, or little over $\frac{3}{4}$*d.* per head.

On the other hand, in the case of intoxicating drugs, Bengal gives a revenue of about £85,000, and Oudh, North-West Provinces, and the Punjaub, £66,000, against only £2500 in Madras and £15,000 in Bombay. In the case of opium, the receipts in Bengal appear to be about £85,000; Oudh, North-West Provinces, and Punjaub, £67,000. Assam and British Burmah each contribute nearly as much as Bengal; while Bombay gives only £17,000, and Madras, according to Government returns, nothing.

It will be seen that Madras and Bombay, which are usually considered rather poverty-stricken districts, and contain only about one-third of the total population of British India, give sixty per cent. of the excise revenue from spirits, and about forty per cent. of the total excise duties.

STAMPS.

THE gross revenue now being derived from the sale of stamps (other than postal and telegraph) is about three millions sterling, and the gross charges about £125,000, leaving a net revenue of over two or three quarter millions. Of this amount nearly two millions are derived from "court fees" stamps, or those used in judicial proceedings. As the total net cost of the administration of "law and justice" appears by the Government returns to be £2,527,000, a very considerable proportion of which must be allocated to the cost of magisterial and judicial establishments for trial of criminal cases, it seems more than probable that the fees charged in civil suits considerably exceed the cost incurred by the State in the settlement of civil disputes; in fact, that the State makes money out of the suitors.

The schedules of the Stamp Act are voluminous, and few transactions in the interchange of property of any description escape this taxation. The rates on mercantile transactions, bills of exchange, etc., are heavy, far exceeding in most cases those charged in England. Documents made in native states are treated as if issued in foreign territory, and where the native state has its own system of stamp duties, they thus come under double impost. For example, the coffee planters in Mysore, whose financial transactions are chiefly with the European houses in the Madras Presidency, repeatedly find themselves subjected to this double burden.

The proportion of revenue derived from the different Presidencies averages as follows :—

Bengal (including all British India except Madras and Bombay)	£2,000,000
Madras	500,000
Bombay	500,000
	£3,000,000

THE MINT.

THE Government of India has mint establishments at Bombay and Calcutta for coinage of the silver and copper coins forming the currency of the empire. Formerly there was a third mint at Madras, but this was abolished some years ago. The receipts of the department, mainly from the seignorage duty on coining silver, average some £180,000 annually, and the expenses of establishment, stores, etc., about £110,000, thus showing a small profit of about £70,000 a year.

PAPER CURRENCY.

THE paper currency of India is managed by the Government, and not, as in other countries, by a State bank.

The currency notes of the Government of India are issued by the Paper-Currency Department, and the issue is regulated by a special Act of the legislature. The main features of this Act are as follows:—Notes can only be issued against a reserve of similar value, of which one-half must be in silver or gold coin and bullion; the other half may be in Indian Government securities (*i.e.* certificates of the Indian public debt). Each Presidency has a separate issue, and each again is divided into Circles. The notes issued in any special circle are legal tender only within its radius; but notes of all sub-circles may be tendered in the central or Presidency circle. The notes of one Presidency are not legal tender in another; but payment of any currency note may be claimed at the treasury of the Comptroller of paper currency in any Presidency town.

The paper currency was instituted in 1862, and the circulation has made satisfactory progress. The average monthly value of notes now in circulation may be taken as eleven millions sterling, and full advantage has been taken of the privilege of holding a portion of the reserve in Indian Government securities. About five and a half millions is so held, and the annual interest thereon enables the department to show, after covering all expenses, a handsome surplus of profit, averaging about £200,000 annually.

SAVINGS BANKS.

THE Government instituted a savings bank system in 1861. The accounts are kept by the Presidency banks, but deposits may be made or withdrawn at any of the district treasuries in the interior by persons residing in the mofussil. No deposit of less than one rupee is received, and no person is allowed to deposit more than Rs. 500 (£50) in any one year, or to have a larger deposit than Rs. 3000 (£300) at one time. Pass-books are issued to depositors, and have to be produced on each occasion of deposit or of withdrawal. The accounts are made up, with interest, on the 31st March of each year. Parents may make deposits in the name of their children while minors; such deposits can only be withdrawn during a child's minority by a legal guardian.

The rate of interest allowed is 3¾ per cent.

per annum. No interest is allowed for broken periods of a month, or on fractions of a rupee. Considering the low rate of interest allowed as compared with those current among the natives of India for small loans among themselves, for which 2 per cent. per month is a common charge, the progress made must be considered very satisfactory. The Government returns show a very rapid increase since the first few years of the movement, the present amount of transactions being about as follows :—

	Number of Depositors.		Amount of Deposits.	
	European.	Native.	European.	Native.
Bengal	3,361	7,113	£149,070	£161,950
Madras	3,001	5,556	77,120	128,018
Bombay	6,447	16,849	203,098	683,933
	12,809	29,518	£429,288	£973,901
	42,327		£1,403,189	
		Average ...	£33 3s.	

Observe that Bombay with much the smallest population shows by far the largest figures. This is of great significance. The Presidency city of Bombay is the only part of India where manufacturing industries have made any progress worth mentioning, and here we have proof how such industries tell on the prosperity of the people.

FORESTS.

Of recent years the Government has given much attention to the conservancy of Indian forests—partly on the ground that previous neglect, or a too facile readiness to permit the destruction of jungle for the purposes of coffee or similar cultivation, has caused extensive denudations of surface, and affected, if not the rainfall, at all events the distribution or storage of the water which falls during each monsoon; partly also with the wish to turn to financial account the valuable property which the State undoubtedly possesses in the timber of the Indian jungles.

It seems very doubtful whether the clearing of the hillsides in the great coffee and tea growing districts has really had the effect on the rainfall which has been asserted to have occurred. In fact, the statistics of rainfall show no diminution of quantity. There is, however, evidence sufficient to warrant the belief that such clearances in the watersheds which supply great rivers have altered the character of those rivers; that the water during the rains comes down in heavier flood, while during the dry seasons it loses volume at an earlier period than formerly. In a country which requires irrigation for its more important crops, effects such as these should not be overlooked.

The Indian Government derives at present a net revenue of about £200,000 per annum from its property in forests. Details of this revenue are about as follows:—

British Burmah		£45,200
North-West Provinces and Oudh ...		52,900
Bombay		60,500
Central Provinces		38,900
Bengal		9,200
Punjaub		5,600
Madras		1,800
		£214,100
Less loss—		
Assam	£3,500	
General expenses of Government of India	8,600	12,100
		£202,000

It is difficult to get accurate statistics regarding the work of the department, the area under its management, and the establishment employed. The whole matter appears at present to be in a transition stage. The Government of India has a "Forest Bill" in preparation, which will define the respective rights of Government and of village communities, and the powers to be given to forest officers; but the subject is a most delicate one to handle, and great care will be needed to avoid confiscation of private rights of practically immemorial duration. There can be no doubt that, under the old Hindoo system, each village community claimed communal privileges over the forests, within certain recognized boundaries; and in this manner, in the more settled and populous districts, it would appear that all forest was appropriated among the several village communities. Each village enjoyed the rights of cutting timber for firewood, for house building, and for agricultural implements, and of collecting various jungle products; and during the hot season, when forage is scarce, it is immemorial usage to drive the village cattle into the jungles, to feed on the grass under the trees and on tender shoots and leaves, etc., etc. It is understood that the Government intends to curtail considerably the extent over which such privileges may in future be exercised; leaving to the villages merely such extent as the forest officers may consider necessary for communal purposes, and demarcating the remainder as Government reserve for the growth of valuable timber, firewood for the railways, etc., etc. Where the country is more thinly or not at all cultivated, the forests are, as a rule, claimed by native rajahs or zemindars, who have a prescriptive or hereditary right of cutting timber, collecting jungle products, etc., and who, in many cases, have parted with large tracts of land, either on lease or by sale of the freehold, to coffee and tea planters and others. It is proposed to restrict, as a measure for the public good, the promiscuous felling of such jungles, more especially near the sources of streams, etc., and to place even admitted private rights under the control, in this respect, of the forest officers.

There are further large tracts over which no distinct private or communal title can be shown, and which are treated as Government waste lands, and these are already under the care of the Forest Department. What extent of forest land actually belongs to Government is not at present accurately known, though it is undoubtedly very large; and still less can it be estimated what additions the measures for further reserves above alluded to will create. It may, however, be considered as certain that the Government has already in hand a source of considerable net revenue, and from all the information which can be procured from forest officers and others capable of arriving at sound conclusions, it seems probable that the returns will, before long, largely increase. Young plantations of teak and other good timber trees have been made, which should in time be very valuable. The writer has seen a calculation which serves to show that the teak plantations of Nellumboor, in Western India (Malabar), will alone be worth some six millions sterling within the next half century. Such calculations, however, must be taken under considerable reserve. Such property, like the future value of the Indian railways and telegraph system, should be taken into account when estimating the future of Indian finance. It is too much the custom to look at the annual statements of Indian revenue and expenditure by themselves, without any notice of the large and increasing value of the State property which is constantly under creation.

The Forest Department is managed chiefly by members of the Uncovenanted Service, under the immediate control of the Collectors of the respective districts.

THE "NATIONAL DEBT" OF INDIA.

THE funded debt of India is at present, in round numbers, about a hundred and fifty-six millions sterling, of which about sixty-seven millions is sterling loan held in England, and the interest payable in British currency, and about eighty-nine millions is "rupee paper," both principal and interest being payable in India in silver. The interest on rupee paper held in England is paid by drafts on the Indian treasuries at Calcutta, Madras, or Bombay, which drafts are saleable in London at the current exchange of the day. The amount of rupee paper held in England may vary greatly; it appears at present to be about fourteen millions sterling. Of the total funded debt it is estimated that about one-third is held by natives of India.

The interest on this funded debt amounts to about six millions.

The empire is further responsible for the interest on the capital of the guaranteed Indian railways; but this responsibility is strictly limited to the deficiency, if any, between the aggregate amount of interest on all capital (about ninety-six millions sterling) of those railways and the aggregate net traffic receipts.

The liability per head of the population of British India in respect of the funded debt amounts to about 16*s.* 1½*d.*, while the incidence per head of the annual charge for interest on that debt does not exceed 8*d.* Even for such a poor population as India's there is nothing very startling in these figures, but, as the writer has pointed out, a large proportion of the funded debt is practically represented by railway property in actual or prospective possession of the State; while for much of the balance there is "cover" in the immense mass of property which has of late years been created by the State, in public buildings, such as Government offices, hospitals, schools and colleges, barracks, etc.; in lines of telegraph, canal and irrigation works; and further in "waste" lands, and forests, and the hitherto undeveloped mineral resources of the country—all which matters may fairly be taken into account when estimates are made of the actual financial position of the empire. And if we further consider that India has as yet hardly touched the great resources of wealth derivable from manufacturing industries; that, instead of adding to her internal wealth and prosperity by such pursuits, she is able to spend some thirty millions annually in buying the productions of foreign countries, we must surely admit that there is no just ground for the despairing opinions which have recently been expressed on the future of Indian finance. Such opinions can only have their rise in the imperfect knowledge which, unfortunately, is too prevalent of India's real position and resources, and must disappear as the British nation becomes educated into a better appreciation of the great value of its Indian dependencies.

CONCLUDING CHAPTER.

In the foregoing chapters I have endeavoured to explain the main principles of the organization which England has created for the Government of India, and to give some general idea of the varied duties which are performed by the executive officers of the Indian services. I now wish, in conclusion, to earnestly impress upon my readers that England's connection with India is no longer that of a trading corporation working for gain, but rather that of a Trustee, with responsibilities involving the happiness and prosperity of an enormous population. And if England is prepared to conscientiously discharge her trust, she must go beyond the daily routine of executive government. So far we have done little more than the elementary work of providing a constitution and the ordinary requirements of civilization; but we must do much more than this if we desire to see the country become wealthy and contented under our rule. Political considerations alone, if no higher principles influence our policy, demand that this further work shall be done. We have undertaken the charge of an estate which possesses enormous, though yet undeveloped, resources, with a population poor beyond any idea which Europeans can readily realize—a population, if not deficient in the means at least deficient in the practical knowledge required to turn the great resources of their country to profitable account; a population of which the great majority are absolutely dependent upon agriculture for a livelihood, and are liable to all the horrors of famine whenever unfavourable seasons interfere with the regular cultivation of the soil. I submit that among the responsibilities which England has accepted in her guardianship of India is the duty of directing and encouraging the natives in the development of India's great mineral resources of coal, iron, copper, lead, which at present, for want of technical knowledge and local enterprise, remain buried and unproductive wealth; in the promotion of improved systems of agriculture which will increase the fertility of the soil; and in the introduction and extension of industrial arts and manufactures. It will, I think, be a surprise to most of my readers to hear that for such simple articles as glassware, crockery, soap, candles, paper and all varieties of stationery, cutlery and all varieties of hardware, all varieties of "haberdashery," matches, clocks and watches, and many similar articles, India is almost entirely dependent upon Europe; although, with abundant cheap labour and material she ought to be able to supply not only her own wants but foreign markets. By far the larger part of the cotton goods she uses are imported from abroad, though two hundred years ago Europe was dependent upon India for cotton goods. With an enormous export of hides and skins, she absolutely imports dressed leather, harness, etc., from Europe. With soils and climate capable of producing the finest tobacco, she pays large sums every year to Manila for cigars, and to America and England for pipe tobacco. Nearly all the chemicals and drugs she requires are imported in a manufactured state, often at great expense; sulphuric acid, for example—a cheap supply of which might be of incalculable service to the agriculture of a country where cattle manure is largely used for fuel, and hundreds of thousands of tons of bones are allowed to rot unutilized every year. And so long as all this remains unremedied England's work in India is still unfinished. It is, no doubt, much to have given the people of India the blessings of security to life and property; still this is but a first step to the full measure of prosperity of which India is capable, and the further progress towards which must greatly depend upon the individual exertions of those who can realize how much the reputation of England is concerned in its attainment. I cannot think that England yet recognizes her duty to India when I see that endeavours to encourage, for example, the local manufacture of cotton goods are regarded in very influential quarters, not with gratification that a profitable and permanent employment is being opened out to scores of thousands of hitherto hard-worked and underfed daily labourers, but with alarm lest Lancashire should lose a market for some small proportion of her vast productions.

Influenced by such considerations as these, and believing, as I do, that the work hitherto completed by England in India is the admiration and the envy of the civilized world, I may be pardoned for expressing my conviction that this further question of the future material progress and prosperity of the country concerns our national honour; and that the indifference of this generation to Indian interests will, if continued, be regarded by posterity as not only a short-sighted blunder in politics and in finance, but as a selfish and unpatriotic neglect of duty—an offence against those principles on which England has hitherto relied to maintain our country's honour, to uphold her influence in the councils of the world, and to extend and secure her beneficent dominion.

APPENDIX.

PRINCIPAL INDEPENDENT NATIVE STATES.

Name.	Area in Square Miles.	Population.	Revenue.
			£
Kashmir	68,000	1,600,000	823,200
Kapurthala	1,650	470,000	170,000
Mandi	1,200	135,000	36,500
Chamba...	3,216	140,000	19,000
Suket	420	45,358	6,775
Bahawalpur	22,000	500,000	200,000
Patiala...	5,412	1,650,000	440,000
Jhind	1,236	311,000	65,000
Nabha	863	300,000	65,000
Kalsia	155	62,000	13,000
Maler Kotla	165	46,200	28,000
Faridkot	600	68,000	30,000
Dujana	100	27,000	60,000
Loharu	285	22,000	6,600
Patandi...	50	21,000	8,100
Nepaul	54,000	2,000,000	1,000,000
Sikkim	1,550	7,000	700
Bhutan	2,000	60,000	
Udaipur...	11,614	1,161,400	64,000
Jeypore	15,250	1,995,000	475,000
Jodhpore	35,670	2,000,000	250,000
Bundi	2,300	224,000	80,000
Kota	5,000	450,000	200,000
Jhallawar	2,500	226,000	160,000
Tonk	2,730	320,000	110,000
Karauli	1,870	124,000	50,000
Kishungurh	724	105,000	130,000
Dholpur	1,600	500,000	110,000
Bharatpur	1,974	743,710	287,500
Alwar	3,000	778,596	230,000
Carried forward ...	246,134	16,042,264	5,118,375

Name.	Area in Square Miles.	Population.	Revenue.
			£
Brought forward ...	246,134	16,042.264	5,118,375
Bikanir	24,000	300,000	102,032
Jessulmere	12,250	75,000	10,000
Serohi	3,200	55.000	11,000
Daugarpur	1,000	100,000	15,000
Banswarra	1,500	150,000	30,000
Pertubgurh	1,460	150,000	60,000
Shahpoora	1,200	133,000	30,000
Gwalior...	33,119	2,500,000	1,200,000
Indore	8,015	635,400	500,000
Bhopal	8,200	769,200	268,340
Dhar	2,500	150,000	80,000
Dewas	2,576	121,800	60,000
Jaora	872	85,500	79.930
Rewa	13,000	2,035,000	250,000
Tehri	2,000	195,000	90,000
Dattia	820	180,000	100,000
Sampthar	175	108,000	40,000
Baroda	4,399	2,000,000	1,150,000
Kohlapore	3,184	802,690	304,720
Sawunt Wari	900	190,814	29.400
Kutch	6,500	500,000	130,000
Hyderabad	98,000	10,500,000	2,000,000
Mysore	27,070	5,055,000	1,029,900
Travancore	5,630	2,311,380	535,000
Cochin	1,360	598,350	130,850
Cooch Behar	1,306	532,565	100,000
Manipur	3,000	126,000	5,000
Tippera	3,867	74,242	18,690
Rampore	945	507,013	146,400
Garhwal	4,180	150,000	80,000
	522,362	47,133,218	13,695,637

MINOR FEUDATORY STATES AND CHIEFTAINCIES.

		Area in Square Miles.	Population.	Revenue.
Northern India ...	20 "Hill states"	6,000	492,000	£ 75,300
Central India.				
Bhopal Agency	21 minor states	2,000	237,000	120,000
Bhopawar "	7 " "	3,000	120,000	40,000
Dhar "	6 " "	2,500	100,000	Uncertain
Gwalior	7 " "	Uncertain	Uncertain	"
Indore Central Agency	15 " "	"	"	"
Malwa Agency...	20 " "	"	"	"
Nimar " ...	7 " "	"	"	"
Various	14 " "	28,000	900,000	48,900
Bundelkund	24 " "	8,655	1,017,000	251,200
Western India.				
Kattywar	26 chieftaincies	Uncertain	1,830,000	1,000,000
Kohlapore	11 "	"	250,000	83,000
Mahikanta ...	28 "	"	150,000	32,000
Pahlanpur... ...	10 "	7,000	530,000	120,000
Rewakanta ...	6 "	4,000	380,000	155,000
Various	59 "	Uncertain	Uncertain	Uncertain
Sattara Jaghirdars	6 "	9,600	570,000	150,000
Southern Mahratta Jaghirdars ...	8 "	2,100	610,000	190,000
Surat Agency ...	3 "	1,050	130,000	50,000
Chota Nagpur (the Tributary Mahals)	9 "	16,500	490,000	Uncertain
Orissa (the Tributary Mahals) ...	17 "	14,900	1,140,000	45,000

INDIAN RAILWAYS.

The following table gives the length of each railway which has been sanctioned, completed, or is in course of construction or of survey :—

RAILWAY.	Gauge.		Length of Line sanctioned.	Portion laid with Double Line.	Length remaining to be finished.
GUARANTEED.	Ft.	In.	Miles	Miles	Miles
East Indian { Main line	5	6	1279½	410¼	—
East Indian { Jabalpur line	5	6	223¾	—	—
Great Indian Peninsula	5	6	1280½	325	—
Madras	5	6	857	42¼	—
Bombay, Baroda, and Central India ...	5	6	421½	23¼	—
Sind, Punjaub, and Delhi { Punjaub and Delhi ...	5	6	553¼	—	—
Sind, Punjaub, and Delhi { Sind	5	6	109¾	4½	—
South Indian	3	3⅜	663	—	—
Eastern Bengal	5	6	159	—	—
Oudh and Rohilkund	5	6	546¾	—	—
Totals for Guaranteed Railways ...	...	...	6094¼	805¼	—
STATE.					
Bengal Provincial :					
Calcutta and South Eastern	5	6	28	—	—
Nalbati	4	0	27¼	—	—
Northern Bengal ... ... {	3	3⅜	239	} —	19½
	5	6	12½		
Tirhut ... ... {	3	3⅜	76¼	} —	—
	5	6	2¾		
Patna-Gya	5	6	58	—	58
Assam	—		—	—	—
Western System :					
Punjaub Northern ... ... {	5	6	173¾	} —	119
	3	3⅜	48½		
Indus Valley	5	6	500¼	—	1¼
North-Western Provinces, Provincial :					
Muttra-Hathras	3	3⅜	29	—	—
Cawnpore-Furrukhabad	3	3⅜	87	—	87
Dildarnagar-Ghazipur	5	6	12	—	12
Central System :					
Rajputana	3	3⅜	419	—	19
Western Rajputana	3	3⅜	299¼	—	263¾
Sindia	5	6	74¾	—	40¾
Neemuch	3	3⅜	303½	—	217¼
Holkar	3	3⅜	86	—	—
Carried forward			2477	—	837¾

RAILWAY.	Gauge.		Length of Line sanctioned.	Portion laid with Double Line.	Length remaining to be finished.
	Ft.	In.	Miles	Miles	Miles
Brought forward	...	...	2477	—	837¾
Native States:					
Gaekwar of Baroda's	2	6	55¼	—	35¼
Khamgaon	5	6	8	—	—
Amraoti	5	6	6	—	—
Nizam's	5	6	121	—	—
Mysore	3	3⅜	—	—	—
British Burmah:					
Rangoon and Irrawady Valley	3	3⅜	163	—	—
Rangoon and Sittang Valley	3	3⅜	—	—	—
Bombay:					
Dhond-Mammád	5	6	145	—	—
Karwar	3	3⅜	—	—	—
Patri	5	6	22½	—	—
Central Provinces:					
Wardha Valley	5	6	46¼	—	—
Nagpur and Chattisgarh	3	3⅜	123¼	—	123¼
Totals for State Railways			3167¼	—	996¼
Totals—Guaranteed and State Railways ...			9261¾	805½	996¼

N.B.—Much of the "Length remaining to be finished" has been completed since these figures were made up.